MORTGAGE FREE *by* 40

A Simple Model for True Home Ownership Early in Life

By Matthew Jeffery

Copyright © 2022 Matthew Jeffery
All Rights Reserved.

This book is geared toward providing reliable information in regard to the topic and issue covered.

In no way is it legal to reproduce, duplicate, or transmit any part of this document in either electronic means or in printed format. Recording of this publication is strictly prohibited, and any storage of this document is not allowed unless with written permission from the author.

The information provided herein is stated to be truthful and consistent, in that any liability, in terms of inattention or otherwise, by any usage or abuse of any policies, processes, or directions contained within is the solitary and utter responsibility of the recipient reader. Under no circumstances will any legal responsibility or blame be held against the author for any reparation, damages, or monetary loss due to the information herein, either directly or indirectly.

Thank you for taking the time to read my book!
If you enjoy the material please leave me a review on Amazon.

For my wife, who asked me to uproot our lives to live mortgage-free.

Thank you.

My journey to mortgage freedom became a reality in 2019 when my wife and I paid off our house. I'll share our story and insights on how living mortgage-free can change your life. *Mortgage Free by 40* offers practical, clear, and useful insights to help people from all walks of life live healthier financial lives.

A home is often the largest purchase most people make in their lives, and while there are ample financial self-help books, this quick read specifically targets eliminating mortgages early in life. Most advice in a home-buying experience comes from banks, mortgage brokers, real estate agents, lawyers, friends, and family that share strategies that are misaligned with long-term financial wellness.

I'll share my experiences as a home buyer and some bad financial choices I made along the way to guide you through the steps toward personal financial freedom. While this short book isn't a silver bullet, I can offer honest and valuable tips that will save homeowners money on their initial purchase and assist with managing financial responsibilities over the life of the mortgage. Simply stated, this is an insider's guide from someone who is living mortgage-free, so you can make informed decisions and get a little closer to that elusive dream we call FINANCIAL FREEDOM.

The best part? This book can be read in a single weekend. Let's roll.

TABLE OF CONTENTS

INTRODUCTION: **Financial Literacy**	7
CHAPTER ONE: **Debt Is the Enemy**	11
CHAPTER TWO: **A Beautiful Mess**	17
CHAPTER THREE: **What Is a House?**	27
CHAPTER FOUR: **Homeownership Club**	35
CHAPTER FIVE: **Compounding Interest**	41
CHAPTER SIX: **Time**	49
CHAPTER SEVEN: **The Contrarian**	55
CHAPTER EIGHT: **Geoarbitrage**	61
CHAPTER NINE: **Leverage**	65
CHAPTER TEN: **Crawl, Walk, Run**	73
CHAPTER ELEVEN: **Liberation**	89
CHAPTER TWELVE: **Bring It**	93
REFERENCES	96

INTRODUCTION:
Financial Literacy

Financial literacy is a major problem in America. The irony: people want to make smart financial decisions even if they don't always do it. At least I want to believe that—I have to believe that.

I read a fantastic blog by OppU that revealed the latest trends in America to better understand financial literacy. The statistics showcase how well equipped we are as a nation to effectively manage our finances. Many of these studies were conducted prior to the COVID-19 pandemic. Obviously, much has changed in our lives, but the information shows that we have the tools to effectively manage our money and make smart business moves in our lives.

Here are some of their revealing statistics on financial literacy in America:

#1: Most adults are financially anxious.

Not only do we have a financial literacy problem, but we're freakin' stressed about it and really don't want to talk about it.

Our financial confidence isn't improving. More than half of surveyed adults say thinking about their financial situation makes them anxious.

Have you ever noticed how most people in our lives (friends and family) are guarded about their finances? The only people that like to talk about money have good news to share! The rest—let's talk about sports or the weather. No . . . fly . . . zone.

#2: Two in three families lack an emergency fund.

According to an analysis from JPMorgan Chase, the majority of families in the US don't have enough money saved in an emergency fund.

Approximately two-thirds of American families are unable to tap into a six-month savings account. Shoot—we're lucky if we can tap into a one-month emergency fund as we're living paycheck to paycheck. A large portion of the population is at risk, which is another source of anxiety, as we're hoping or assuming nothing will happen that will require us to tap into the fund. If you have kids that run, roofs that block rain, or cars that go vroom-vroom, then I assure you, you will need an emergency fund. With financial devastation one unexpected event away, this statistic emphasizes how critical building an emergency fund is for long-term financial and mental health.

#3: The majority of adults live paycheck to paycheck.

This one hurts me. Over half of the nation is living paycheck to paycheck. Simply stated, living paycheck to paycheck means you are spending your income on expenses with nothing left for emergency funds, college accounts, or Disney trips.

Those stuck in this hand-to-mouth cycle often feel like prisoners to their financial condition. What happens if a job is lost or savings runs out? Again, another source of anxiety to manage.

#4: Three in five adults don't keep a budget.

In 2019, a Consumer Financial Literacy Survey revealed three in five American adults self-reported that they do not adhere to a household budget.

How could you possibly know how well or poorly you're doing financially without keeping a budget? My wife has always been better at budgeting than me and, therefore, always had a beat on what expenses we could afford. Good on her, bad on me.

This is a fundamental tenet of financial literacy, and without a budget, you're flying blind and asking for a financial disaster.

#5: Student loan payments are crippling Americans.

In 2020, student loan debt reached a record high of $1.56 trillion. Holy guacamole, that's a lot of dough! These debt obligations are crippling Americans, especially once they secure jobs that can only incrementally pay down these debts. These debts were created in just a few years and can remain for decades. Is government education loan forgiveness the answer? I will refrain from providing an opinion, but this measure shows the magnitude of this debt crisis.

While options such as loan refinancing, consolidation, and forbearance can temporarily ease the pain, the debt balance is always there, lurking in the background. Stressful.

#6: We have credit card debt.

Every day we get closer to a cashless society, but based on the amount of plastic swiped every day, we have successfully generated a record in credit card debt exceeding $1 trillion, according to our friends at the Federal Reserve.

No need to elaborate further here, as you'll quickly learn my thoughts on credit card debt in chapter 1, "Debt Is the Enemy."

#7: Fewer than one in five adults are confident in saving.

How do we know if we're saving enough? Enough for retirement, enough for the Land Rover, enough to send our kids to college?

Few of us feel confident about our savings patterns. The primary worry is retiring with enough money. If we know this is the primary area of worry, why don't we save more for retirement?

Stagnant wages, priority confusion, stock market performance, and competing expenses, among others, are to blame.

The takeaway from these inspiring statistics? We struggle with navigating financial literacy, and I struggle with it as well. Each one of these areas deserves its own book, but we're going to zero in on the single greatest source of household debt and a subject we all need to be financially literate on — mortgages.

CHAPTER ONE:
Debt Is the Enemy

Common terms in nearly every business, university, and government office are cut and *reduce*, often under the auspices of politically correct verbiage, such as *right size* or *realignment of resources*. From the United Kingdom to Italy to Greece and the United States, the major Western democracies are struggling to keep their economies in optimal working order. These world powerhouses are willing to pump trillions into their economies while disregarding debt levels along the way. This addiction to debt has unfortunately trickled down to their citizens. The levels of personal and government debt have become a societal failure. Consumers and politicians are in a spiraling debt cycle with no end in sight or desire to correct the problem.

The US national debt hit a record level of $30 trillion in 2022. The US breached the 100 percent debt-to-GDP mark in Q3 2020 to combat the new coronavirus, and tax revenue was declining. We haven't experienced public debt levels like this since World War II.

While $30 trillion is a staggering number, the annual estimated interest payments on this debt level are also noteworthy:

Fiscal Year	Interest on Debt (in billions)
2018	$325
2019	$375
2020	$376
2021	$378
2022	$399
2023	$428

Source: Fiscal Year 2021 Budget Proposal

What Happens in Debt Crisis

A true debt crisis occurs when a country is in danger of not meeting its debt obligations. A debt crisis is a situation in which a government (nation, state/province, county, or city, etc.) loses the ability to pay back its governmental debt or incrementally service the interest payments. When the expenditures of a government are more than its tax revenues for a prolonged period, the government may enter into a debt crisis. Various forms of governments finance their expenditures primarily by raising money through taxation. When tax revenues are insufficient, the government can make up the difference by issuing debt (treasury notes, bills, and bonds).

The first sign is when the country finds out it can't get a low-interest rate from lenders. Investors become concerned that the country can't afford to pay the bonds and will default on its debt. That happened to Iceland in 2008. It threw the country into bankruptcy. Debt default has also occurred in Argentina, Russia, and Mexico in modern times. While Greece was bailed out of its crisis by the European Union in 2010 to stave off a greater effect, it has repaid only a fraction of the money it was loaned.

Individuals, businesses, and countries all experience debt crises. However, a country has a significant advantage over individuals and businesses—it can print its own money. Cutting expenses, which is an excellent strategy for you to get out of debt, might be politically unfavorable for a country to resolve its debt crisis.

Household Debt Crisis

A household debt crisis occurs when a family starts falling behind on monthly mortgage payments and other personal items that have been financed. Common types of household debt include the following:

- Home mortgages, including both first and secondary mortgages, and home equity lines of credit
- Credit card debt (also called *revolving* credit)
- Auto, furniture, and student loans (also known as *non-revolving* credit)

Any sudden loss of income—or an increase in costs—can cause a household debt crisis. The biggest cause is medical expenses, which generate half of all bankruptcies in the United States. Other causes include extended unemployment or uninsured losses.

A household debt crisis can also creep up slowly. One cause is poor debt management, such as only paying the interest on credit cards. Another is economic change, such as when the housing crisis occurred in 2008. Many homeowners had teaser rates that reset after the first year. The housing bubble was caused by runaway mortgage investment practices on home loans with a high risk of default.

Some owners had planned to sell their home before the crisis, but then the house was worth less than the mortgage. Another troubling example is families who get in over their heads with education loans. The price of education keeps going up, and parents don't want to tell their children they have to drop out or not go to college.

Settling Household Debt

Once a household debt crisis occurs, there are three common ways to resolve it. First, improve your income position through a second job/promotion or selling assets such as a home or a vehicle. Second, cut expenses. That includes switching to a lower-interest-bearing credit card, using cash instead of credit, driving a paid-off vehicle, canceling cable, stopping eating out, and reducing shopping. Third, declare bankruptcy and start over. I guess there is a fourth: receiving a bailout from a friend or family. None of these options are fun.

National Debt Crisis Solution

The solution to the debt crisis in the US is economically easy but politically difficult: agree to cut spending and raise taxes. Who just laughed out loud? Have you noticed that neither Democrats nor Republicans have an appetite for these strategies, even during strained financial periods like now? In 2020, Federal Reserve chairman Jerome Powell went on record stating the government will provide unlimited liquidity until the pandemic is under control. At this juncture, there appears to be no end in sight to government debt accumulation, even as inflation begins to rise above national targets.

Personal Debt Crisis Solution

While I will briefly drown you in national trends, it should be noted that **mortgages are the single greatest source of debt that can be controlled with proper discipline and strategy.** This book looks at mortgages and money from different perspectives, from choosing your loan to what to do when you have fully paid off your home. Many people consider their mortgage a life sentence—I did in 2017. I'm here to tell you that it's not, and with a well-thought-out plan of attack, you'll fully own an appreciable asset that will generate further wealth for you and your family.

Many homeowners start with a thirty-year mortgage amortization (how long it will take to fully repay the mortgage), but nothing is stopping you from paying your mortgage off sooner. As you'll soon learn, there are many simple things you can do in your everyday life to be mortgage-free.

I aim to inspire you to grab the mortgage bull by the horns and take control of your finances. This book isn't just about buying a home and paying it off sooner; it's about financial freedom and, more importantly, personal freedom. It's time to rethink how you view money and to reshape your finances. Debt sucks—and you deserve a life without that burden.

CHAPTER TWO:
A Beautiful Mess

First things first—this book is brief, occasionally irreverent, and will constantly beg you to stop being stupid. As you might expect, the material is centered around financial independence. That's the last time I will use the term *financial independence*, as I find it ambiguous and cliché. A more fitting term is *personal freedom*, which is truly what we're striving for through eliminating debt in our lives. So, let's try this again; this is a book centered around getting closer to personal freedom by living mortgage-free. The aim is to accomplish this goal early in life (around forty years young). Does this imply that hope is lost for someone in their fifties and beyond? Of course not. The principles addressed are applicable for any age, but the earlier you can ditch these interest-sucking leeches we call *mortgages*, the better off you'll be. We'll also cover some important macroeconomic trends, unconventional strategies for generating wealth, and silly habits that get in the way of living mortgage-free.

Homeownership has been and will continue to be a large part of the American dream. I think it's safe to say that the goal of property ownership is a dream shared by most in the world and not limited to the American populace. It was once common to accumulate the necessary capital to purchase a house without a loan. I'll have to trust the historical lore on this concept, as it's been absent in my lifetime. The term "ownership" has become a misnomer and a word that warrants further analysis. We've come to accept ownership as closing on a house at a title company. You know that celebratory day where you sign a pile of paperwork, keys are exchanged, you are provided garage door openers, and maybe you popped a bottle of champagne. Congratulations, you're a homeowner! You put down 3–5 percent and are now $300,000 (or worse) in debt. You don't "own" squat, silly rabbit.

As an economics student in the early 2000s, I was intrigued by the numbers analyzed by government and academic institutions. Gross domestic product (GDP), unemployment rates, inflation, opportunity costs—fancy terms all trying to explain how and why the economy behaves under certain market conditions. I'm not going to test your knowledge of supply and demand curves, but we do need to take a beat and analyze the housing market.

"Homeownership" rates have increased steadily since the peak of the last housing crisis. The median FICO score for an originated mortgage rose from 707 in late 2006 to 765 in early 2021.

Despite the credit requirement increases from 2006 to today, banks are beginning to yet again relax lending standards criteria. The chart showcases a slow but steady credit score increase since Q1 2003.

Credit Score at Origination: Mortgages*

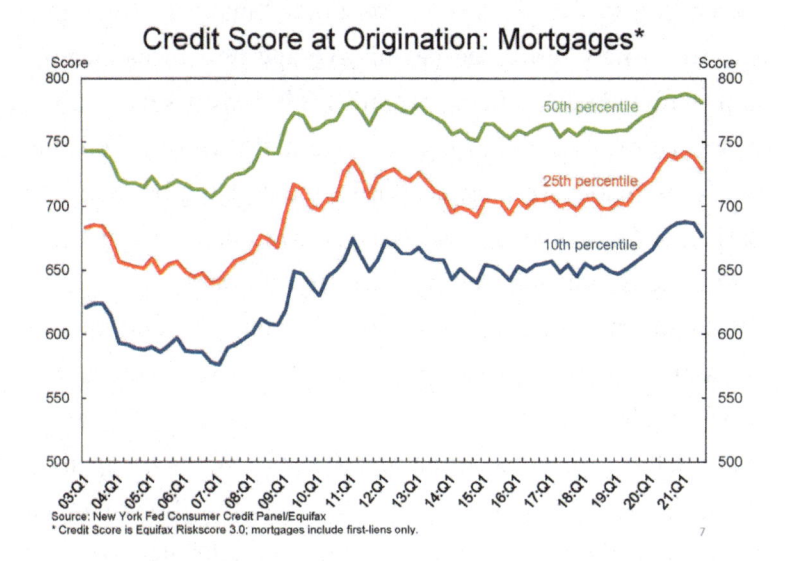

Source: New York Fed Consumer Credit Panel/Equifax
* Credit Score is Equifax Riskscore 3.0; mortgages include first-liens only.

This trend is outstanding. Let's give ourselves a back slap.

Not so fast. We'll dive into quantitative easing shortly, but this credit score easing has enabled more people to qualify for bigger home loans. Would you take the complimentary business class upgrade even though you know your budget better aligns with coach? Of course you would! Ever heard these lines: "You've worked hard for this," or "You and your family deserve this." Banks are in the business of making money and are not your friends; stop being stupid. Banks and their predatory practices get their own chapter. Just because you're technically eligible for a loan based on bank assessments of FICO, income, low-interest rates, and debt levels, it doesn't mean you should take the bait. Banks continue to screen customers based on debt-to-income ratios (DTI), but because of more lax lending standards and low interest rates, customers are taking on bigger loans than ever before.

According to data from the Consumer Financial Protection Bureau, a new mortgage has an average unpaid balance of approximately $260,000. Overall, DTIs have risen over the years. Home loans showed a slow but steady rise from the 1980s, with a sharp increase during the housing boom of the early 2000s. The financial crisis of 2008 created a drop in momentum, but only temporarily, as DTIs are approaching pre-financial crisis levels. COVID-19 is ongoing and interest rates are rising as I write this book. This worldwide health crisis is affecting the broad economic market and housing market, likely in a discerning way. Or is it? Will lending standards tighten up again as experienced after the 2008 financial crisis, or will banks continue to lend with unbridled avarice? I'm going with unbridled avarice, not just because it's fun to say and was used in the *Christmas Story* movie, but the banking industry and general population can't help themselves, especially when "cheap" money is available.

This cheap money comes in the form of favorable interest rates attached to mortgages, which thus far has made the housing market surge. Yes—interest rates are lower, money is cheaper to access, but the debt continues to compound.

With rates now rising, where does the mortgage debt fit within the overall debt balance composition?

Total Debt Balance and its Composition
Trillions of Dollars

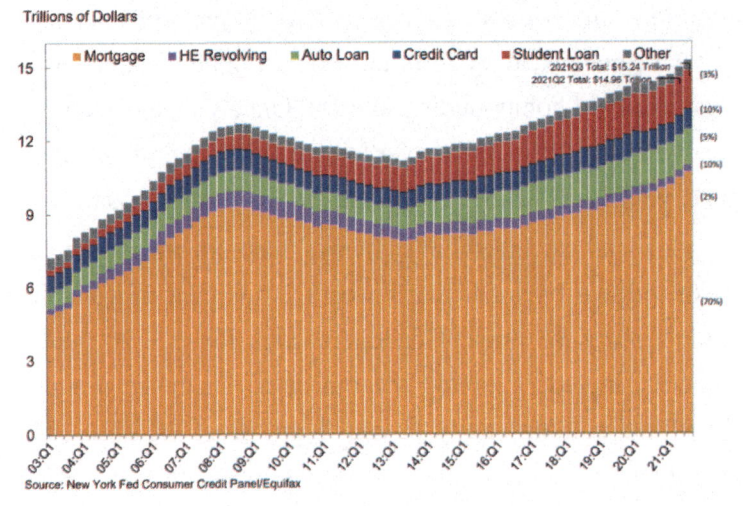

Legend: Mortgage, HE Revolving, Auto Loan, Credit Card, Student Loan, Other
2021Q3 Total: $15.24 Trillion
2021Q2 Total: $14.96 Trillion

(3%)
(10%)
(5%)
(10%)
(2%)

(70%)

Source: New York Fed Consumer Credit Panel/Equifax

That's right, mortgages (by far) sit as the #1 source of debt for households, representing 70 percent of the total debt balance. Consider what your life might look like if you wiped this burden off the books. I get it; it's too painful to think about when it's not a plausible reality. The primary drivers behind larger loans are escalating home prices, a healthy Wall Street economy (in late 2021), lower down payment requirements, and credit score easing practices. Historically, the average down payment on a new home purchase was 6 percent. That's right, 6 percent, while the other 94 percent is rolled into the loan, ready to compound interest for the next thirty years. Warren Buffet speaks of compounding interest in his book *Ground Rules* (great read, by the way), and those who understand its mechanics greatly benefit, while those who don't will surely lose. I assure you that all lending institutions have a crystal clear understanding of how compounding interest works in their favor. Don't hate the player (banks), hate the game. In defense of banks, you are solely responsible for securing that large loan and becoming a prisoner to 30 years of interest. If you have one takeaway from this book, I hope it's a better understanding of compounding interest. Once you understand all the money you're handing over to banks over the life of a mortgage, you'll want to live mortgage-free as fast as possible.

Financial advisors have always recommended that you make a down payment that's worth 20 percent of your new home's purchase price. General reasons for this 20 percent objective include avoiding the mortgage insurance premium (MIP) and gaining equity in your home from the onset. This 20 percent goal is unrealistic for most households for various reasons. These include low savings levels, high home sales prices, or investing capital elsewhere (cars, college, vacations, 401K). Many homes of today are purchased with only 1-2 percent down!

More than six million home sales occurred in 2019. Statistics show a steady increase in new and existing home sales. In 2011, the total number of house sales was 4.75 million. That is a 26 percent increase within that eight-year period. This data provides further evidence of lax lending standards, a robust economy (teetering now), and a yearning for homeownership, no matter the cost to the personal balance sheet.

Real estate plays a pivotal role in the US economy. In 2018, real estate construction contributed approximately $1.15 trillion to the nation's economic output. That's 6.2 percent of US gross domestic product. Those are some serious numbers, so it should not come as a shock that the government plays such an active role in lending practices. Home sales are great for the economy and will continue to be one of the most measured metrics in evaluating the nation's economic health. While construction is the only part of real estate that's directly tied to gross domestic product, real estate affects other areas of the economy that are not directly measured. A decline in real estate sales eventually leads to a decline in real estate prices. When real estate prices fall, this has a direct effect on home equity and available capital to tap into via home equity loans. Consumer confidence is also impacted by falling real estate prices driving families to rent versus "buy." Understandably, people get skittish in declining housing markets, as housing is typically viewed as an appreciable investment choice. By extension, a depressed housing market drags down the entire economy. And by further extension, a depressed economy is lousy for our investment portfolios, re-election chances for our national leaders, and overall consumer confidence.

When consumer confidence turns negative, people stop consuming. This is a real problem that contributes to a downward spiral in the economy. More depressing events such as rising unemployment and loan defaults could ensue. Scary stuff, right? When news of a teetering economy is imminent, the Federal Reserve often intervenes by reducing interest rates through QE (quantitative easing), investing in national infrastructure projects, and flooding the market with liquidity to make borrowing and access to money easier. The government literally increases the money supply—out of thin freakin' air. These are really the only tools that governments have consistently used to stabilize faltering economies. As such, national debt levels due to overspending and stimulus packages are at record highs.

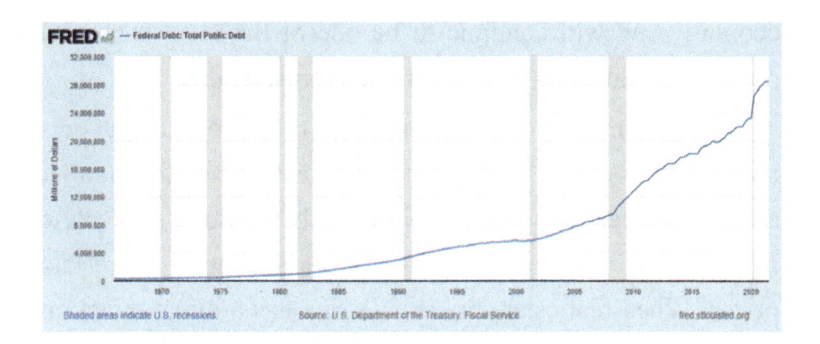

Real Estate and the 2008 Recession

There's no better example of real estate's impact on the economy than the 2008 financial crisis.

Falling home prices initially triggered the spiraling economic domino effect, but few realized it at the time. According to the National Association of Realtors, by the summer of 2007, the median price of an existing single-family home was down 4 percent since its peak in October 2005. Call it what you want—a recession, bear market, or flawed investment bundling practices leading to the collapse. I was living in Tampa, Florida, one of the hardest-hit areas, during this period and watched property values drop 30 percent. It felt like it all came collapsing down without warning, leaving homeowners in disarray by the sudden negative turn of events.

For perspective, many compared it to the decline during the Great Depression of 1929. Many also likened it to the decline of the oil industry in the early 1980s. I didn't personally experience those events, but by those standards, the slump was barely noteworthy but significant for those who experienced the effects.

Various economic studies showed that national average housing prices declined between 10 percent and 15 percent. These losses were enough to eliminate homeowners' positive equity position. Those were the realities experienced in Florida, Nevada, and Louisiana. Many books and movies have been made covering these events. Simply put, it was ugly.

Death by Derivatives

Almost half of the loans issued between 2005 and 2007 were subprime. A subprime mortgage is a loan that's issued to borrowers with an impaired credit history and carries a higher interest rate. Sometimes, the borrowers have no credit history to assess default risk, thus warranting higher interest rates to mitigate risk. Conventional loans are generally not an option in this lending space due to poor FICO scores, previous default history, and low income. The real problem was that banks used these mortgages to support large sums of derivatives. Large sums as in the trillions. Banks folded the subprime mortgages into these mortgage-backed securities. They sold them as investments to other investment houses/corporations and were buried in 401K balances.

When borrowers defaulted, the mortgage-backed securities value was negligible, resulting in unsurmountable losses to the banks. The Federal Reserve ended up bailing out these financial institutions. If you were around for these events, you remember the line, "Too Big to Fail."

Banks with lots of mortgage-backed securities on their books, like Bear Stearns and Lehman Brothers, were in big trouble. Lehman Brothers went bankrupt, which officially kicked off the 2008 financial crisis. In the end, more banks should've defaulted, but this reality posed too great a risk to the overall economy, so they were bailed out. Can you say golden parachute?

Is Another Crash Looming?

The stock market has been artificially propped up for years through government intervention via tax cuts, low-interest rates, and ballooning federal spending. Interest rates have been low, enticing borrowers to take the loan bait. Something has to give, as this path is unsustainable. Update! Inflation in 2022 is soaring throughout the world, including the United States, leading to rising interest rates. Surprise, surprise.

The economic effects of COVID-19 will likely be experienced for years as Main Street workers will need to secure additional capital to offset job losses, loan defaults, and lost business income due to closure.

As you can see, selling homes is a big deal in the US and other nations and serves as a representative pillar for economic health. It, therefore, comes as no surprise that the government and loan-issuing banks want to make lending easily accessible in this high-stakes game. Unfortunately, playing this game comes at a monumental price to the buyer—to you.

CHAPTER THREE:
What Is a House?

The typical new American single-family home has become increasingly luxurious. Newly-built houses in the US are some of the largest in the modern world, and their size-per-occupant has nearly doubled in the past fifty years. Let's compare average square footage over the last fifty years.

- 1970s: 1,600 square feet
- Current: 2,600 square feet

The number and size of the rooms are also growing and taking on other purposes, such as art rooms, libraries, and even gymnasiums. The mansions of the '70s would be the "typical" new homes of the 2020s. I have childhood memories of knocking on our single bathroom door because it was "my turn." Those were the days!

But why do we need this much space? Don't worry, I'm not going to push tiny houses on you, but I do commend those that embark on this form of minimalism and decluttering their lives to find more via less space. My general hypothesis for the growing need for more space is a juxtaposition of easy credit, social norms around materialism, privacy from family members, and living in a tangible representation of success (that's right—ego). As the new houses have become more luxurious, homeownership itself has become a luxury. Young adults (under forty) today are one-third less likely to own a home at this point in their lives than previous generations. Among young black Americans, homeownership has fallen to its lowest rate in more than sixty years. Are young adults worse at managing money than previous generations? I don't believe this is the case, but these realities are common by falling into the above-mentioned money traps.

The most expensive housing markets, such as San Francisco and Los Angeles, haven't built nearly enough homes for the middle class, driving prices up due to scarcity. As urban living has become too expensive for workers, many of them (including yours truly) have either stayed away from the richest, densest cities or moved to the South and West, where land is cheaper. While denser cities offer more job opportunities for workers, the mortgage expectations are crushing our abilities to become true homeowners. Instead of growing as they grow richer, New York City, Los Angeles, and the Bay Area are all shrinking. These are really cool cities (in my humble opinion) with very large housing problems. Easy solutions are tough to come by, especially when viable housing alternatives exist in mid-market cities.

Lastly, and the most dangerous philosophy of all, is if I can buy more through lending, I should, since housing prices typically appreciate. Therefore, the larger my base starting point, the greater the return. This is a BIG MAYBE, as there is no guarantee your home will appreciate in value. My first two homes I sold at a loss. Yes - both homes depreciated in value. The only guarantee with this strategy is your personal balance sheet will become weighed down in debt, pushing you further away from personal freedom.

> "A nation of homeowners, of people who own a real share in their own land, is unconquerable,"
> - *Franklin D. Roosevelt said in 1942.*

This FDR quote should not be interpreted as a nation of homeowners need to buy huge houses, but public policies derived from Fannie Mae, Freddie Mac, and the Federal Housing Administration are all directly aimed at augmenting loans and moving properties. In addition, zoning mandates of municipalities propelled the development of suburbs, which provided for more bang for the buck by purchasing on the outskirts of cities.

Ironically mid-twentieth-century suburb homes were modest in size, roughly 850 square feet. But through time, public policy, mass-produced building materials, aggressive marketing, and people regarding their houses as investments versus homes reshaped the sizing landscape as we know it today.

Across the country, the supply of housing hasn't kept up with population growth.

Single-family-home sales are stuck at mid-'90s levels. The undersupply of housing has become one of the most important stories in economics in the past decade. In 2010, one might have thought that the defining housing story of the past century would be the subprime fiasco that plunged the US economy into a recession. But the past decade has been defined by the mix of the excessive luxury-home building with the cratering of middle-class-home construction. The future might restore a measure of sanity with another large market correction. But for now, the nation is pricing the middle class out of the large metropolitan areas.

So how much space is really necessary for your family? Larger houses indeed offer more bedrooms, bathrooms, formal dining areas, and rooms for an air hockey table or in-home movie theater rooms. Smaller houses require smarter organization and have lower overhead expenses from heating, cooling, home furnishings, and cleaning.

Lifestyle, rather than size dimensions, is often the driving force behind home square footage decisions. Factors such as family size, entertaining habits, access to local amenities, and proximity to work and schools all influence lifestyle. While all these factors deserve careful consideration, I recommend tremendous focus be placed on "affordability." Does lifestyle preference take priority over affordability, or vice versa? There probably is a balancing act happening during this assessment.

Don't look at what your friends and family live in, and definitely do not look at what celebrities live in. These reference points can serve as an incredible disservice to your home buying decision-making.

The Affordability-Needs Tradeoff

One obvious constraint against more square footage is the relatively higher price of bigger homes.

Some buyers want what they want and are willing to pay a premium to accommodate their desires. I highly discourage this, and you will leave a lot of money on the table embracing this approach. I encourage you to tailor your "true" needs for a right-sized home that fits within your personalized budget. Do you really need the in-home gym that adds 350 square feet to your purchase price when a public gym is a half mile down the road?

Watch some reality TV shows and you're sure to hear: "I love the living-room space. It's perfect for entertaining," "The master bedroom is huge," or "Walk-in closets are a must." This is house porn. I'm not here to tell you to hate nice things, but what are you trading on the affordability front?

How Many Square Feet Do I Need?

As you consider your next home, many questions come to mind. What's the best location? Do you want a sprawling ranch or a traditional two-story home? Would a condo be best? Whether you are considering buying an existing home or contacting a luxury home builder to design a new one, one of the top questions you must consider is size. Exactly how much square footage do you need for your family?

There is much to consider in answering this question. Use the following tips to guide yourself through this process.

Bedrooms vs. Living Space

The two main areas of the home are the bedrooms and the living areas. What should you look for to achieve a good balance of bedrooms and additional space for living? A good rule of thumb is to ensure there are places for nearly every family member to sit in the dining room and living areas. This will help provide a good balance to the home and allow room for eating and relaxing.

We're not in the 1960s, and our fast-paced lifestyles reduce full family dinners at the formal table. And how often does the entire family hang out in the living room together, staring at their phones? Those couches sit vacant 80 percent of the time. Wasted space and furniture.

Current Needs vs. Future Needs

Consider whether this is a home that you will be living in long-term or a starter or temporary residence. You may only need space for two adults now, but you may plan to have kids in the future. If you don't want to move again, it might be worthwhile to plan enough square footage to house children down the road. If your mother-in-law might eventually move in, you'll need a room for her as well.

Luxuries vs. Reality

As you work out your budget for square footage, consider what spaces you will actually use. Some homeowners plan out a gym, a theater, and a formal dining area that add significantly to the square footage of the home. Of course, these also add significant costs. Decide what areas you will actually use. Be honest and realistic about your true needs. Is it worth the extra cost to add a gym, or would a treadmill in the basement be just as good? Perhaps your money would be better spent on extra square footage for a play area that will get more use.

Lifestyle vs. Budget

Finally, you'll have to be realistic about your budget. Even if you determine you need 4,500 square feet, this size might not match your budget. Go back to the previous item and weigh which areas you truly need and will use the most. Focus on creating extremely functional and enjoyable spaces in those areas to maximize your budget and get the best fit for your family's lifestyle.

CHAPTER FOUR:
Homeownership Club

My wife and I, after paying off our mortgage in 2019

After four mortgages in three cities, my wife and I traded a $360,000 mortgage for a paid-off house. As you can see from the above, we were pretty pumped after paying off our remaining mortgage balance. Our formula was simple: we capitalized on a market opportunity and were able to make this dream a reality.

Before I go further on the personal story, let me share my thesis on paying off properties. Anyone can do it as long as there is discipline in the process, and read carefully here: IT HAS TO BE A TOP PRIORITY IN YOUR LIFE.

Let's dive into some more data.

Approximately 38 percent of owner-occupied households in the US are completely paid off, or said another way, 62 percent of owner-occupied households hold an interest-sucking mortgage.

Mortgage-free homeownership is higher among low-income families and in small cities with low housing costs than high-income families in large cities, according to a new study by Construction Coverage, a Los Angeles-based construction content website. Say what? That's right, mortgage-free homeownership is HIGHER with lower-income households versus higher-income households.

Surprisingly, mortgage-free living is more common for homeowners who make less than $25,000 a year. Some 54.5 percent of low-income Americans have paid off their homes, outpacing the national average by 16.5 percentage points, although they are less likely to own a home overall. Meanwhile, homeowners with a six-figure salary tend to face higher mortgage payments relative to their income. I'll say it again, say what? Shouldn't it be easier to pay off a mortgage when the salary is higher? This is the paradox of DTI evaluation methods leading us astray in our purchasing habits.

Small and mid-sized metro areas outperformed the average. In mid-sized metro areas with under 350,000 residents, like Odessa, Texas, and Charleston, West Virginia, 49.2 percent and 47.5 percent of homes are paid off, respectively. Housing costs represented only 16 percent of income in each city, about half of the threshold to be considered burdened by housing costs.

And mid-sized metro areas with fewer than 1 million residents, like McAllen, Texas, and Brownsville, Texas, had 49.6 percent and 47.9 percent of homes paid off, respectively. Housing costs occupy only about 20 percent of the personal balance sheet for each metro.

The bottom falls out in large metros with over one million residents, as fewer homeowners have paid off their homes. New Orleans, Detroit, Houston, and San Antonio are the only large cities with at least 30 percent of owner-occupied homes paid off—still falling short of the national average by as many as 8 percentage points. Most large American cities are struggling to achieve these statistics.

Mortgage payoff rates vary substantially across demographic groups. While at the national level the share of homeowners under age sixty-five who have paid off their homes is 26.4 percent, certain demographic groups have much higher or lower rates of free-and-clear homeownership. Being mortgage-free is strongly (negatively) correlated with both household income and home value. Higher-income households with higher-valued homes are less likely to have their mortgages paid off, and many households who have paid off their mortgages live in areas with lower costs of living.

Comparing age groups, people aged nineteen to twenty-five are more likely to have paid off their mortgages than people aged twenty-six to forty-four, but the rates of homeownership among this age group are obviously much lower. The same phenomenon is present when looking at educational levels among homeowners. People with less than a high school degree are much less likely to be homeowners, but those who do purchase homes are more likely to be mortgage-free.

At the state level, West Virginia and Mississippi have the largest rates of free-and-clear home ownership at 41.3 and 39.4 percent, respectively. Louisiana, North Dakota, and New Mexico also have large percentages of paid-off homes. At the low end, Maryland and Massachusetts have the smallest shares of residents who have paid off their homes, at just 16.6 and 19.2 percent, respectively.

West Virginia and Mississippi have the largest share of "free and clear" homes

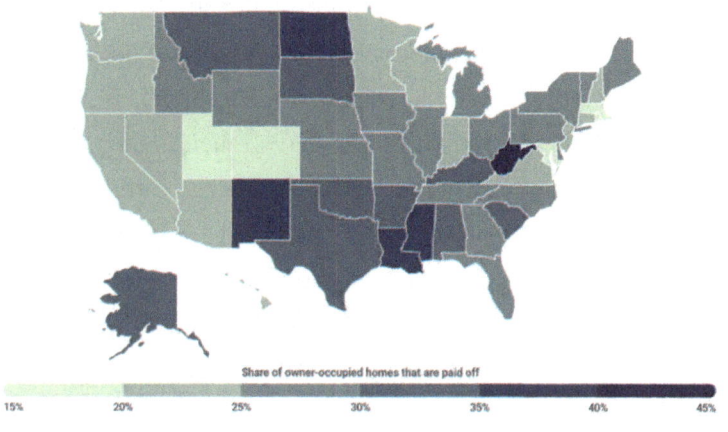

Share of owner-occupied homes that are paid off

15% 20% 25% 30% 35% 40% 45%

Source: U.S. Census Bureau's 2018 American Community Survey Public Use Microdata Sample

There are a few takeaways here I would like to reinforce further.

1. More affordable houses (with all the bells and whistles we want) are found in less densely populated cities.
2. A positive correlation exists between income levels and housing debt levels since banks are willing to lend more based on higher income.
3. Individuals with lower income levels are achieving greater success in paying off their homes.

It's empirically verified that homeownership is buoyed by debt, as the share of owner-occupied homes paid off doesn't breach 50 percent in any state. If this doesn't bother you, then you should probably stop reading this book now. If you find this alarming, then let's continue with the most crucial topic in this book—compounding interest.

I almost forgot to share my personal story of debt-free homeownership! I wish I could tell you it was through highly disciplined saving, living off packaged ramen noodles, and working three jobs to get there. Nah, I was a putz that got himself head deep in debt by buying a large home in Colorado and borrowing against my 401K to eliminate the mortgage insurance premium (stupid move). My wife and I were paying $2,800/month and on the thirty-year payoff plan. My roots saved me. We had recently had a baby and chose to move back to our home state of Oklahoma to be closer to family. Our rental property had exponentially appreciated, and we sold it for a large profit. Profits were used to buy a house in Oklahoma. We capitalized on a market opportunity and pursued geo-arbitrage. As detailed in the Liberation chapter, we also played the "used" game to our advantage - used cars, furniture, toys, cooked at home most of the time, and limited vacations. We were partially lucky, but also strategic by choosing to live in a location where our dollars had stronger buying power. We'll dive into why I'm a huge proponent of geoarbitrage soon—but first, compounding interest.

CHAPTER FIVE:
Compounding Interest

Compound interest is the 8th wonder of the world. He who understands it, earns it, he who doesn't, pays it.

- *Albert Einstein*

My wealth has come from a combination of living in America, some lucky genes, and compound interest.

—*Warren Buffet*

This is the most important topic in this book and why millions of people never live debt-free. On the flip side, compound interest is the reason people find financial independence and can exponentially expand their wealth.

We're going to approach this chapter utilizing the economic principle of *opportunity* costs. By definition, *opportunity costs* means "the loss of potential gain from other alternatives when one alternative is chosen." For example: if I have $1 to spend at the local grocer, choosing between a $1 pack of gum or a $1 soda and I select the pack of gum, the opportunity cost is I don't get the soda. That's cool; I gave up soda a long time ago. These choices happen in life all the time as we have limited financial resources at our disposal. We must make spending choices and live with the resulting opportunity costs. Unfortunately, we often make choices that are detrimental to our financial health and ability to live mortgage-free.

The most common mortgage is the thirty-year fixed-rate mortgage. In summary, the borrower pays a set (fixed) interest rate for the thirty-year life of the loan. Benefits include certainty of payment terms and making monthly payments more affordable since the loan is stretched out over thirty years. As further enticement, interest rates have been at historic lows through early 2022 but are on the rise to combat rising inflation.

What Is an Amortization Schedule?

An amortization schedule is a table that provides the details of the periodic payments required to gradually pay off the home loan. Through these payments, the principal of an amortizing loan is slowly paid down over the loan term. Typically, an equal amount of payment is made every month. Of course, it can't be that easy, as real estate taxes, which are lumped into the loan payments, fluctuate, affecting the monthly payment amount. You might have noticed that real estate taxes rarely go down, so your "fixed payment" actually increases based on these tax adjustments.

An amortization schedule can be generated by an amortization calculator, with the inputs of the amount, periodic terms, and interest rate of the loan. Through amortization schedules, borrowers can better plan and track how much they still owe and the time horizon to fully pay off the loan.

Understanding Amortization Schedules

Periodic payments are made for amortizing loans, such as a car or home mortgages. Each payment consists of two components: the *interest charge* and principal *repayment*. The percentage of interest or principal repayment varies for different loans.

The amount of interest charged for each period depends on the predetermined interest rate and the outstanding balance of the loan. The remaining portion of the periodic payment is applied to repay the principal. Only the portion of the principal repayment reduces the remaining loan balance. Typically, the remaining balance of an amortizing loan diminishes as time passes, with principals repaid. Thus, the interest amount for each period also decreases over time, and the principal repayment increases gradually.

Example of Amortization Schedule

Consider a $30,000 fully amortizing loan with a term of five years and a fixed interest rate of 6 percent. If only more houses were this affordable! Payments are made on a monthly basis. The following table shows the amortization schedule for the first and last seven months.

Month	Total payment	Interest	Principal	Ending Balance
0	-	-	-	30,000.00
1	579.98	150.00	429.98	29,570.02
2	579.98	147.85	432.13	29,137.89
3	579.98	145.69	434.29	28,703.60
4	579.98	143.52	436.46	28,267.14
5	579.98	141.34	438.64	27,828.49
6	579.98	139.14	440.84	27,387.66
⋮				
54	579.98	19.90	560.08	3,420.06
55	579.98	17.10	562.88	2,857.18
56	579.98	14.29	565.69	2,291.49
57	579.98	11.46	568.52	1,722.96
58	579.98	8.61	571.37	1,151.60
59	579.98	5.76	574.22	577.38
60	579.98	2.89	577.09	0

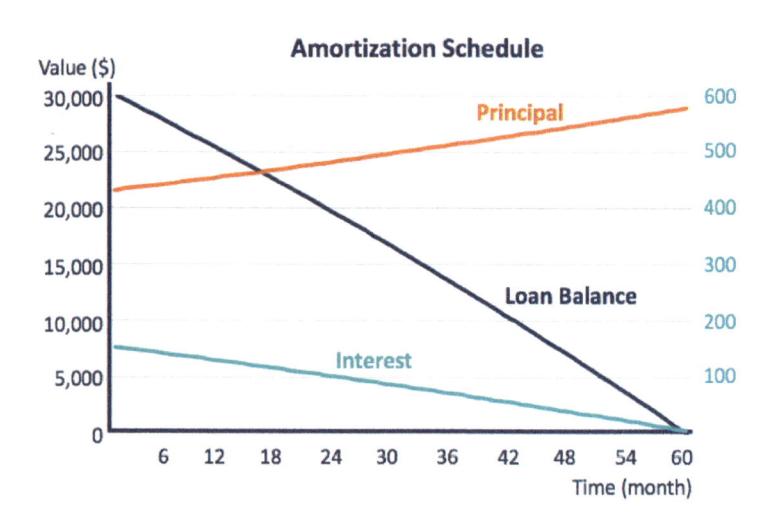

The loan is fully amortized with a fixed total payment of $579.98 every month. The interest payment for each month can be calculated by multiplying the periodic interest rate with the ending balance from the last month. The remaining portion of the total monthly payment is thus the principal repayment.

In the first month, $150 of the total payment is the interest, and $429.98 is the repayment for the principal, which reduces the balance of the loan. As time passes, the interest portion decreases, and greater values are applied to the principal. The balance of the loan, therefore, diminishes at an increasing speed.

Methods for Amortization Schedule

There are multiple methods to amortize a loan. Different methods lead to different amortization schedules.

1. Full Amortization with Fixed Rate

The full amortization with fixed rate, is where the total interest amount is distributed equally over the life of a loan. It is a commonly used method in accounting and home loans due to its simplicity. With a fixed periodic total payment and interest amount, the principal repayment is also constant over the life of the loan. Again, real estate taxes should be taken into account and will influence this reality.

Pause - for the record, I label the rest of these loan types as gimmicks.

2. Full Amortization with Variable Rate

Fully amortized loans can also have a variable interest rate, which is why they are called adjustable-rate mortgages (ARMs). For example, a 5/1 ARM could have a typical

30-year repayment period with a fixed rate for the first five years, and then its interest rate can change once a year after the initial 5 year period. When the rate changes (up or down), the loan is "re-amortized", and a new amortization schedule is generated. As a result, you'll still pay off the loan in 30 years, but your payments may increase (or decrease) when the loan's rate changes. Considering the rate variability we are now witnessing, is this a good idea? I'll let you answer that rhetorical question.

3. Full Amortization with Deferred Interest

Some partially amortized loans may include interest-only payments for a set period of time before transitioning to fully amortized payments for the remainder of the term. For example, if a loan had a 30-year term, the first 5 years might only require the client to make interest payments. After that, principal and interest payments would be made for the remaining 25 years or until the loan was paid off. Some home equity lines of credit (HELOCs) may have an interest-only period followed by a fully amortized repayment period.

4. Partial Amortization with a Balloon Payment

While uncommon, there are also some partial amortization loans that follow interest-only payments with a balloon payment at the end of the schedule. Can you say kicking the can down the road? Balloon payments were more common with consumer mortgages before the 2008 housing crash and may still be available to some borrowers. But keep in mind, a balloon payment is often tens of thousands of dollars. If you're considering a loan with a balloon payment (which I do not recommend), you'll need to consider whether you can make the balloon payment at the end of the schedule.

5. Negative amortization

In the negative amortization method, the total payment of a period is lower than the interest charged for that period. It means that there is nothing left from the periodic payment to repay the principal, and the remaining interest charge will accumulate to increase the outstanding balance of the loan. The loan balance increases over time and will be repaid at maturity. Terrible idea.

Source: Lending Club

Bringing It All Together

Exhilarating stuff, right? Let's analyze a real-life example. For simplicity, we won't buy any interest points or build in real estate taxes. At the time of writing this book, the average American home is $272,000. Let's say you put 3 percent down and mortgage the remaining $263,840.

Mortgage amount: $263,840

Payoff date: August 2052 (30-year fixed)

Monthly payment: $1,112.36

(payment will go higher due to real estate taxes)

Total interest paid: $136,609.63

Price + Interest = $408,609.63

(Calculated at bankrate.com.)

This is how banks get rich, and you stay poor. **That $272,000 house actually cost you $408,609.** The house is 50 percent more than what was agreed to at closing! Imagine redirecting these interest payments into your 401K, college savings, or starting your own business. I get it; these loans are often the only way to buy a home because few people have $272,000 to buy a home outright. With that said, there are strategies to end this mortgage misery before 2052.

CHAPTER SIX:
Time

I think it's safe to assume most of us want some finer things in life, but is it really necessary to have them? Sure, a big house with multiple bedrooms, a swimming pool out back, an expensive luxury car in the driveway, designer clothes, and other things that suck wealth is what most people aim for. But those "champagne wishes and caviar dreams" can quickly become a disturbing personal weight when it comes to the true cost of ownership.

As previously mentioned, people with a bucket-load of money still manage to drive themselves into the ground. Many superstar athletes who've made millions lose it all, blowing it on nonsense material possessions and other frivolous endeavors. So it's not the money per se but how you spend it that determines your ability to achieve personal freedom.

Would you be happy if you worked two jobs yet still didn't make enough for a decent meal? Do you really want to stay poor? So where is the middle ground? Consider how you spend your money. Luxury cars, massive homes, extravagant vacations, designer clothes, and jewelry all suck wealth and have a short lifespan in delivering happiness.

You might be happy driving your new Porsche for a few months, but the exhilaration will fizzle out after a while. For the record, I'm currently driving a 2014 Subaru Outback with 105,000 miles on it. Rather than dumping a ton of cash on a Rolex, why not be satisfied with a reasonably priced athletic watch that tracks fitness goals? I paid $30 for a LetsFit athletic watch, and it's going on three years now.

The worst part about keeping up with the Jones's is that it can become addictive and eventually leave you knee-deep in debt—or bankrupt.

Expensive and Material Things Can Lead to Slavery

If you keep indulging in luxurious items to satisfy your cravings, you will eventually end up poor. Stop being stupid with these purchases.

> **The things you own end up owning you. It's only after you lose everything that you're free to do anything.**
> *- Chuck Palahniuk, Fight Club*

The worst part about this kind of behavior is that it can be addictive. There is always going to be something more expensive that you wish you had, even though you have enough. According to Ruth Engs, an applied health sciences professor at Indiana University, shopping can actually release endorphins and dopamine in your brain. These hormones and compounds do create a **temporary** sensation or "high" of happiness.

Notice the word I bolded? *Temporary*. Temporary highs lead to recurring needs of release, making you a slave to material items. This pattern can be deadly to your balance sheet and mental health. So how to control these impulses to buy? Hobbies. And, no, shopping is not a hobby. Some recommendations include:

- Cycling
- Walking/running
- Volunteering at a nonprofit
- Writing a book, like I'm doing right now
- Learn to code
- Yadda, yadda

There are endless possibilities to occupy your time and deny these buying impulses before they are allowed to surface.

That's our entire economic system: buy things. Everybody buy. It doesn't matter what you buy. Just buy. It doesn't matter if you don't have money. Just buy. Our entire civilization now rests on the assumption that no matter what else happens, we will all continue to buy lots and lots of things. Buy, buy, buy, buy, and buy. Then buy a little more. Don't create, or produce, or discover—just buy. Never save, never invest, never cut back—just buy. Buy what you don't need with money you don't have. Buy like you breathe, only more frequently. Stop being stupid. Allow your neighbors to be the stupid ones that embrace this *buy* philosophy.

What's More Important—Time or Money?

Money:
- It's hard to earn and easy to spend. We've trained ourselves to believe in the scarcity of money and spend our whole lives chasing it.

Time:
- Time is the scarcest asset in our lives.
- It cannot be replicated or bought. A second gone is lost forever. Stop wasting it.

Freedom:
- I suppose *freedom* is a relative term now; someone is freer than the other based on their circumstances.
- But NO ONE is absolutely free of circumstances. You are as free as you "think" you are!

Successful people utilize their time to the fullest. The one to manage time the best will win. Elon Musk uses time-blocking to assign time blocks to a particular task that he needs to accomplish on a given day. This time-blocking method can be used for any task, ranging from eating a healthy diet, writing emails, scheduling meetings to meditating, or anything that you would like to do on a particular day.

Time is something you can never get back once it is gone, and it's the one thing that can't be stopped or changed. Your time should be the most important commodity you have, and it should be managed well.

You've heard the old adage, "Time waits for no one," and it's going to keep moving at the same velocity whether you want it to or not. Because time won't wait for you. It becomes much more of a scarce resource because every day, we lose some of it. You have to make sure you do what you can to seize every opportunity and make the most of your time as much as possible. Your life and career are governed by time, so stop waiting around for things to happen to you!

We are generally really bad in the way we manage our time. We have limited time at work and at home, so we need to make sure we manage it efficiently. Don't put things off until tomorrow if you can do them today. Seize the moment, and you'll be surprised by how much you can accomplish.

Distractions

Every company wants to be a priority and make you think their product is the most important. Car companies, electronic companies, Amazon, YouTube, and even the water heater repair person that needs a four-hour "appointment" window wants to convince you their product/service is paramount to your existence. There are so many distractions in the world these days that threaten our time. These activities must be managed to ensure our time is appropriately allocated.

Some general tips on time management:
- Utilize weekly schedules—prepare on Sundays
- Ensure personal time is built into schedules
- Prioritize activities to ensure the most important items are completed
- Ensure a time limit is established for each activity
- Establish a consistent weekly cadence

Ready for the irony? Time management is a myth. No matter how organized we are, there are only twenty-four hours in a day, and sometimes, random shit happens that throws our schedules into turmoil. Accept it, internalize it, and move on.

Having a structured time management plan will allow you to stay calm when the most unthinkable disasters descend upon your life.

Never forget—time—once it's gone, it's gone.

CHAPTER SEVEN:
The Contrarian

Entrepreneur and investor Navil Ravikant eloquently stated, "A contrarian isn't one who always objects—that's a conformist of a different sort. A contrarian reasons independently, from the ground up, and resists pressure to conform."

The word *contrarian* is derived from the word *contra*, which literally means "against." The term is often used in the investment sphere when one buys shares of stock when most others are selling and sells when others are buying. These people can be unpopular. It's like the bettor at the craps table betting against the roller on the no-pass line. If you do this in Vegas, you'll likely be heckled, but in the end, it's your money to manage.

Being a contrarian is having enough gumption not to follow the herd and reject conventional social norms. This is tough, and I promise you will be subjected to ridicule for taking the path less traveled.

Contrarian wisdom is constantly surfacing in politics, religion, economic market paradigms, ideological social shifts, and even our focus area of homeownership. You may not view homeownership as a contrarian behavior, but based on the economic and social realities we've previously discussed, I certainly would.

Okay, let's dial this back in. While buying a home is an exhilarating experience full of pride and excitement, getting to pay for that home over the next twenty to thirty years is something . . . ahem . . . shall we say, less memorable. But you can become mortgage-free and be the contrarian.

I think we all can agree that homeownership rocks, but mortgage payments suck. Luckily, there are things you can do to pay off your mortgage faster than the typical thirty year nightmare plan. Ditch the luxury cars, massive homes, designer clothes, credit card debt, and other things that suck wealth, so you can truly buy a house—live the contrarian life.

Change Your Lifestyle

You should be able to spend two or three years living minimally. No more holiday spending, fewer luxuries, and a real focus on spending can result in increased savings. These savings can then be used to make a capital repayment toward your mortgage, taking you a step closer to the end goal. Need specifics:

Holidays: No presents. Choose quality time and a nice holiday meal instead. Never said this is going to be easy :)

Fewer luxuries: Put restrictions on Amazon orders, limit eating out to once a week (at a reasonable restaurant), and forget designer clothes.

Cars

Let's zero in on tier 1 cars. I'm talking about new luxury-brand cars. I know they are nice, but vehicles are one of the worst places to invest your money. They are depreciable assets, and the asking price for these tier 1 cars is simply absurd. I currently drive a 2014 Subaru Outback with 105,000 miles on it. It's paid off and serves its purpose—getting from point A to point B. Stop being stupid with cars. Remember, a $400 car payment is $400 less you can pay down on your mortgage principal.

Sell Any Unwanted Belongings

Most of us have hundreds of dollars of unwanted belongings lying around the house that we don't use or need. Go through every room in your home and set aside anything you think may have some value. Selling online has never been easier, and there could be money to be made. Whether it's children's toys or old mobile phones, it all adds up. Not only will it give you some passive income, but it will also help declutter your home. Contrary to what my three year old son believes - cleanliness is close to godliness.

Throw Away Your Vices

Addictions just aren't worth it. Smoking and large amounts of alcohol are unhealthy and will drain your bank account. Smoking a pack of cigarettes a day will cost you $2,011 a year. According to the Bureau Labor of Statistics, the average American consumer spends $1 on alcohol for every $100 they spend.

Also, Americans are charged more for alcohol than many other nationalities. From 1982 to 2011, there was a 79 percent increase in alcohol pricing in restaurants and bars. Next time you go out to eat or to socialize, try ordering a sparkling water instead. You'll be surprised how much your bank account (and your gut) will thank you for it.

Cable

Who needs cable when you have Amazon Prime and Hulu? I'm not here to endorse Amazon or Hulu but rather simply ask you to run the math on ditching cable for a skinnier TV programming option. I have the light Hulu package and currently pay $13/month and have learned to be satisfied with its offerings.

Work More to Earn Your Beautiful Home

Time is perhaps the hardest sacrifice you can make to save for your mortgage. Most people would rather be doing something other than working; however, picking up an extra shift here or there will pad your wallet. This extra income, when not spent frivolously, can make a significant impact on your savings toward paying off your montage. Finding odd (gig) jobs and ways to make extra money is also an excellent idea to help your savings.

When you have a goal, you can get consumed by it, which can be healthy if the goal is to live mortgage-free. Everything becomes a matter of what would happen if I put another $5 down this week. Embrace the challenge. Any time you get some extra money, the bulk, if not all of it, can go to the mortgage fund.

Mortgage-free living can change your life. Keep in mind that if you want to have a mortgage-free life, you need to be patient, work hard, and make sacrifices in order to reach your goals. Sacrificing your regular lifestyle is hard, but I can assure you, trading some habits for living mortgage-free is a trade you should take any day of the week.

You will take some hits being a contrarian, as you're going against the flow, but exercising restraint in your life in exchange for living mortgage-free is a trade you should embrace. It should also be noted that while you'll be subjected to some ridicule by family and friends, you'll be the interesting one in the pack. Everyone wants a paid-off house, so why not be that person that actually does it?

Yoda would say, "A defacto financial advisor you have become."

CHAPTER EIGHT:
Geoarbitrage

Second to Compounding Interest, this is the second most important topic in the book and will absolutely bring you closer to personal freedom. I was into geoarbitrage before I even knew there was a name for it. I'm sure you're aware that certain parts of the nation are cheaper than others. Simply put, your dollar goes further in less densely populated cities where housing supply is in balance with demand. Let's break it down.

What Is Geoarbitrage?

Geoarbitrage is the act of moving from a high cost of living area to a lower cost of living area to save money. Housing is the number one expense for most people, so finding a way to lower that expense is a great way to save a lot of money and focus on building wealth.

Why Geoarbitrage?

There are a ton of reasons to go geo, especially if you want to embrace frugality, reach your financial goals, and live mortgage-free. In addition to lower housing prices, tax advantages, more space, and fewer crowds are leading reasons for relocating geographically.

The biggest benefit of geoarbitrage is the copious amounts of money you can save on living expenses. The ability to keep more of what you make is the number one reason why relocating to a Southern or Midwestern part of the United States is ideal. There was absolutely no way I was going to achieve financial independence living in Denver, Colorado. I actually lived in a Denver suburb but don't have the heart to call it out, as my wife and I created incredible memories and made lifelong friends. But the one thing I did not enjoy was real estate prices—and it just keeps getting worse. This is not just a Colorado problem. This home pricing assault is occurring across the nation—primarily along the coasts. To place this in context, my wife and I earned respectable salaries, and we still had to take out a 401K loan to ensure mortgage insurance was eliminated from our mortgage. Bad financial move! Even after that terrible financial decision, we still had a $2,800 monthly house payment to manage for the next thirty years. Absolute nonsense. We were never going to pay off that Colorado home, which made me angrier every day I lived there.

After having our first child, my wife delivered a monologue to me at 2:00 a.m. while nursing our son that would've impressed the likes of Shakespeare. She convinced me to take a different job in Oklahoma, move closer to family, and geoarbitrage us to the extreme. Now I live in a small town in the US, with a relatively low cost of living, no mortgage, excellent schools, and am living a great life. The money saved from no mortgage is greatly accelerating our savings and investments portfolio.

Unfortunately, houses are just not affordable in some of the hottest US markets. According to Redfin, the average home price in Los Angeles is currently a whopping $800,000! That is the *average* sale price. Boulder, Colorado, is on par, and Boston sits at $700,000.

In comparison, Savannah is just $111 per square foot. You can buy a very nice house in that city for less than $250,000. There are still places in the US where you can buy a house for under $150,000; I live in one of them. If you want to pursue financial freedom but think it's out of reach due to home prices, consider geoarbitrage. It's guaranteed you'll have friends or family give you a rib punch over how "uncool" some of these places are, but I encourage you to do your own research before accepting their biased commentary.

Taxes

A lot of people choose to geoarbitrage to states without income taxes, like Texas or Florida. Others just try to find areas with low property taxes. Chicago has some of the highest property taxes in the country at 7 percent. Los Angeles sits at 6 percent (granted, 6 percent of $800,000 is much more than 7 percent of $276,000, the average home price in Chicago). In comparison, the average property tax rate in Savannah is only 1 percent. And I'm no math genius, but 1 percent of $250,000 is way cheaper than either of those other options.

Crowds

Lower cost of living areas tend to have fewer people. This has been a freaking huge advantage for me! I can go into almost any restaurant and be seated in less than thirty minutes. Adios, two-hour wait times! Road traffic is more controlled as well. Unless there's an accident, I can get to wherever I need to go in less than a half hour. No more spending my life in traffic. I actually thought I'd have a hard time adjusting to life in a smaller city. Small towns can be just as lively as big cities. Another big bonus is that I was able to buy a home right in the middle of a cool college town. I have a grocery store, an excellent elementary school for my son, and a few restaurants within a stone's throw away.

Only you can decide whether geoarbitrage is right for you or not. It's right for me because I want to decrease my costs as much as possible in order to achieve personal freedom, and I've been fortunate enough to find good jobs in the cheaper areas. COVID remote-working has helped. It's also right for me because my family is in the general vicinity. Your situation and your values may differ.

Personal freedom is the desire of every individual not only in the US but all over the world. Every person wants to reach a point in life where they can afford most of life's goodies with less strain and hassle. With the rising cost of living in most cities in the United States, geoarbitrage becomes an option to fundamentally change the financial game for those people willing to risk it. There are many ways through which you can unlock personal freedom. However, since experiencing it firsthand, geoarbitrage is a highly effective way to quickly change your financial standing.

If you are tired of paying those hefty expenses every month and wish to change your financial status quo, then I encourage you to target small to mid-market cities.

CHAPTER NINE:
Leverage

Leverage is one of the more interesting and difficult concepts to fully grasp in all of finance, but it's important for anyone who borrows or plans to borrow money to understand. Much of the confusion stems from the contrasting meanings embedded in the same word. Included are two very different definitions. The first suggests strength: "power, effectiveness." The other, on face value, has little to do with control: "the use of credit to enhance one's speculative capacity." Combining the two suggests that the party that borrows has the leverage—they have the power and advantage over others. Does that mean that the borrower is dominant over the lender? Somehow, that flies in the face of what many of us learned at an early age. The gambler who can't pay his bookie ends up with the right hook to the gut. Yet many people jump into risky financial situations without considering the potential consequences.

The most intimate relationship most of us have with leverage is our home mortgage. In the vast majority of cases, over many decades, this structure has been positive and transformative to the buyer. However, there are two conditions necessary for financial leverage to actually become powerful. The first is that the borrower must be able to make timely payments or risk repossession. The second is that the asset underlying the leverage holds or increases its value. This game works in the borrower's favor when homes appreciate, but without these conditions, the music stops, and the benefit of leverage becomes a huge liability.

Leverage can be positive, thanks to the countless individuals and businesses in existence who have relied on a loan to get started. Leverage can and does work under the right circumstances. Lending would not still be in existence after thousands of years if it wasn't a useful tool. But careful analysis and preparation by the borrower of several possible scenarios—good and bad—for the business, project, or investment are necessary to really know what you're getting into. Otherwise, debt will be your worst enemy.

Leverage: Why You Need It & How to Use It

Building wealth requires you to work smarter rather than harder by applying the following principles of leverage:

- **Financial leverage:** Passive income coupled with excess capital after all expenses are paid.
- **Time leverage:** Allocated time to advance education and self-advancement that is not earmarked for an employer.
- **Systems and technology leverage:** Other people's systems and technology so that you can get more done with less effort.

- **Marketing leverage:** Other people's online social networking platforms, newsletters, radio shows, and databases so that you can communicate to millions with no more effort than is required to communicate one-on-one.
- **Network leverage:** Other people's resources and connections so that you can expand beyond your own.
- **Knowledge leverage:** Other people's talents, expertise, and experience so that you can utilize greater knowledge than you will ever possess.

Leverage allows you to build more wealth than you could achieve alone by utilizing resources that extend beyond your own. It allows you to grow wealth without being restricted by your personal limitations. Leverage is the principle that separates those who successfully attain wealth from those who don't. It's just that simple.

How to Save Money and Accumulate More Wealth

Financial freedom comes to the person who knows how to save 10 percent or more of their income throughout life. One of the smartest things that you can ever do for yourself is to develop the habit of saving part of your salary, every single paycheck. Individuals, families, and even societies are stable and prosperous to the degree to which they save money. Savings today are what guarantees the security and the possibilities of tomorrow.

Here are the ways to help you save money, accumulate wealth, and increase financial leverage.

Pay Yourself First

Begin today to save 10 percent of your earnings, off the top, and never touch it. This is your fund for long-term financial accumulation, and you never use it for any other reason except to assure your financial future. The remarkable thing is that when you pay yourself first and force yourself to live on the other 90 percent, promoting frugal living, you will soon become accustomed to it.

You are a creature of habit. When you regularly put away 10 percent of your earnings, you soon become comfortable living on the other 90 percent. Many people start by saving 10 percent of their income and then graduate to saving 15 percent, 20 percent, and even more. And their financial lives change dramatically as a result. So will yours.

Take Advantage of Tax-Deferred Savings and Investment Plans

Because of high and even multiple tax rates, money that is saved or invested without being taxed (deferred) accumulates faster than the money that is subject to taxation due to compounding.

Become a Lifelong Student of How to Save Money

Read the best books, take courses, and subscribe to the most helpful magazines - there are plenty out there. Know what you are doing so you can always make intelligent decisions when you invest your funds. Truly indoctrinate your mind with sound money literature and education. Personal freedom comes to the person who actively takes control of their finances.

Tips to Advance Financial Leverage:

1. Begin to Think Positively about Money

Part of becoming rich involves thinking positively about money. Thinking negatively about money is an emotional obstacle that you must eliminate in order to achieve financial freedom.

You must eliminate the thoughts that having more money leads to evil or that money can't buy you happiness. Sure, these items solely won't lead to unequivocal happiness, but when you begin thinking positively about money, you will attract opportunities and open up more doors than you ever thought possible.

2. Rewrite Your Major Goals for Financial Freedom

Set financial goals for yourself. Rewrite and review your goals as necessary and think of how you can accomplish them. This will take you less than five minutes per day, and it's time well spent.

The very act of writing and rewriting your goals and thinking about them each morning before you start off will increase your chances of accomplishing them.

3. Plan Every Day in Advance

Plan every day in advance. The best time to do this is the night before. The very act of planning each day in advance will make you far sharper and more precise at everything you do.

You will find yourself with better focus and a greater sense of self-control and personal power when you work from a list. When you plan every day in advance, you will be better able to control and track your spending habits as well. Plan how much you have to spend for the week, the month, the year, and decide where you will be able to save.

4. The Principle of Concentration

The principle of concentration is absolutely essential to achieve personal freedom. Your ability to develop the habit of concentration will do more to ensure your personal finance success than perhaps any other skill or habit you can acquire. The things you focus the most on and spend the most time doing should be in direct alignment with your financial goals. Highly recommend yoga and meditation as methods to improve concentration.

5. Invest in Yourself

Listen to audio programs in your car. The average person spends five hundred to one thousand hours per year behind the wheel. By turning your car into a university on wheels, you can become one of the most knowledgeable and most skilled people in your profession. Purchase courses on money management, personal finance, and debt management. Very soon, you will have so much knowledge in the area of money that friends and family will come to you for advice.

6. Ask Yourself These Magic Questions

As yourself two "Magic Questions" at the end of each day. The first question is, "What did I do right?" And the second question is, "What would I do differently next time?" Reviewing your performance immediately after each day allows you the opportunity for fast self-correction.

By reviewing what you did right and what you would do differently next time, you program into your mind a predisposition to be even better the next time round. If you take a few minutes and write down everything you did right and everything you would do differently, you can learn and grow in your personal discipline. Evaluating yourself in this manner will cultivate a culture of self-discipline and constant improvement.

So by choosing to focus on money goals that motivate you, while also embedding a positive mindset toward money, yourself, and life in general, you will help to achieve both increased wealth and happiness. And when you get there, evidence clearly shows us that being generous with our money makes us happier—and richer! Saving money is important, whether you're creating an emergency fund or working toward a long-term goal, like paying off your mortgage.

Having enough capital to quit a job, take a lower-paying job, or take time off to be with family is financial leverage. Like compounding, those who maximize their leverage through financial discipline aim to gain greatly. Those who don't will be slaves to their jobs and protract their retirement date. So, I ask you, who is going to have financial leverage in your life?

CHAPTER TEN:
Crawl, Walk, Run

When you start thinking about buying your first house, it's easy to let your emotions run the show. Before you know it, you're stalking homes for sale on your home-browsing app, rearranging your schedule so you can do drive-by viewings, and researching creative financing options that would allow you to buy a house with next to nothing down.

It's all too easy to land on a house you can't afford, and that mistake can affect your ability to build wealth in the long run. But understanding the steps of the home-buying process empowers you to make smart decisions about your home purchase.

How to Buy a House

Buying an affordable house takes time. And no house—not even that perfectly cute bungalow on the corner with the fenced-in backyard is worth jumping into before you're ready. Do you know what's more important than the house you buy? How you buy that house—the process. The decisions you make in the home-buying process can make a difference between a home that's a blessing to your family for years to come and a home that becomes such a financial burden that you feel like you can't breathe. Buying a house doesn't have to be a stressful, draining experience. It can actually be a lot of fun—especially if you're making smart decisions that focus on the long term.

When to Buy a House

First, how do you know it's the right time to buy a house? Before you even think about starting the steps of the home-buying process, there are a few things you should do:

- Evaluate your finances. Make sure you have a consistent income and a good chunk of cash for a substantial down payment. Buying a house before you're ready can lead to financial disaster.
- Consider the housing market. If you want to make a smart investment on your home purchase, you need to buy a house that'll go up in value. Talk to your real estate agent about home values in your preferred area and their potential.
- Think about your life stage. It doesn't make sense to buy a house if you may move next year. The process of buying and selling a house is expensive, so make sure you feel confident you'll be in that area for the next five to seven years to allow appreciation to occur.

If you think it's the right time to step into homeownership, here's how to get started!

Step 1: Save for a Down Payment

It's tempting to skip the money question and jump straight into looking at homes in your area. After all, home shopping is way more fun than thinking through your finances! But a weak financial foundation is a recipe for regret when it comes to your home purchase. Don't shortchange your future by having a short-term perspective. You'll build years of memories in your home. You'll share countless meals in the kitchen and spend hours enjoying warm summer days in the backyard. Do you want those moments overshadowed by financial stress? A home is probably the biggest purchase you'll ever make. Are you sure you're ready?

Answering the following two questions will help you know!

Are You Financially Ready to Buy a House?

Before you begin the home-buying process, I recommend paying off other debt and saving up three to six months of expenses in an emergency fund. Being financially ready to buy a house is important.

When you no longer have a landlord, the responsibility of paying for repairs falls on you. So what happens if your water heater bursts after just three months in your new home? Lived it! When you don't have room in your budget and no savings to fall back on, you may be eating ramen for the rest of the month to get that fixed. But if you have a full emergency fund and no debt taking up "real estate" in your monthly budget, an unexpected repair won't rock your whole life.

How Much Should You Save?

Just like any goal, buying a home the smart way takes planning and preparation. The most time-consuming task is saving cash for the down payment, closing costs, and other moving expenses.

- **Down payment:** I recommend putting down at least 10 percent on your new home, but 20 percent is even better because you avoid private mortgage insurance (PMI). That's an extra cost added to your monthly mortgage payment, and it doesn't go toward paying off your mortgage balance.

- **Closing costs and prepaid:** Closing costs are the fees charged by title companies and lenders involved in your real estate transaction. Prepaids cover any prorated property taxes and insurance items.

- **Moving and other expenses:** Moving expenses can vary from hundreds to thousands of dollars depending on how much you're moving and how far away your new home is from your current place. To help with budgeting, you can call moving companies in your area for quotes ahead of time. If you plan to make updates to your home—like repainting, installing blinds, or buying new furniture—you'll need cash for that, too.

Ready to get your savings rolling? You've got this! Saving for a down payment isn't rocket science. Set a plan and focus on your milestones, and you'll have that down payment before you know it. You've got what it takes!

Step 2: Get Preapproved for a Mortgage

The best way to buy a home is with cash. It may sound crazy, but people like you do it every day. If that's not feasible for you, you'll need a home mortgage loan.

Before we move on, I would like to address a principle that some famous financial educators have addressed in their multistep process to financial wellness. They have couched a mortgage as healthy debt. Nonsense. It's debt, and all debt has a detrimental effect on your bottom line and personal freedom. If you can pay off your house, do it. Do not let concepts surrounding tax benefits from property taxes and mortgage interest cloud your mind or that your money will make a better return if invested in the stock market. You *might* make more money in the stock market with that capital, but there are no guarantees. When you choose to pay off a house, you are guaranteed to have a paid-off house. Forever. Period.

Remember our chapter on opportunity costs? Every mortgage payment makes the bank richer, reduces investable income, and protracts your time horizon for true financial wellness. Okay, let's continue the conversation on mortgages (if they're absolutely necessary).

How Do You Get Preapproved?

In a quick conversation with you about your income, assets, and down payment, a lender can prequalify you to buy a house. Getting preapproved takes a little more work. A lender will need to verify your financial information and submit your loan for preliminary underwriting. But it pays off when you begin your home search because a preapproval letter shows that you're a serious buyer.

How Do You Know Which Mortgage Option Is Right for You?

Bad financing turns your biggest asset into a liability. That's why getting the right mortgage is so important! Setting your boundaries on the front end makes it easier to find a home you love that's in your budget.

Here are the guidelines I recommend:

- A fixed-rate conventional loan: With this option, your interest rate is secure for the life of the loan, leaving you protected from rising rates. Any other mortgage option is a terrible idea.

- A fifteen-year term: Your mortgage payment will be higher with a fifteen-year term, but you'll knock out your mortgage in half the time of a thirty-year term and save thousands in interest.

- Monthly payment of no more than 20 percent of your monthly take-home pay: This leaves plenty of room in your budget to achieve other goals, like saving for retirement or putting money aside for your kid's college fund.

Once you know how much you can afford to spend on your new home, stick to it. And if you're buying a home with your spouse, make sure you're both on the same page about your budget. Reread that last sentence - I can't reinforce it enough.

Step 3: Find the Right Real Estate Agent

Though your search for homes may start online, it shouldn't end there. You can do a lot of research on your own, but you need the help of an expert when it comes to finding and securing your perfect home.

A buyer's agent can help you navigate through the home-buying process. In some cases, they may even be able to help you find a house before it hits the market, giving you a competitive edge. And when it comes to making an offer, your agent will negotiate on your behalf, so you don't pay a penny more than you have to.

How Does a Buyer's Agent Get Paid?

A real estate agent will advocate for your best interest and is a crucial part of your home-buying team. But they don't work for free. So how much should you be prepared to pay?

How Does Nothing Sound?

In some cases, the seller pays your real estate agent's fees, so using a buyer's agent is "free" to you. In reality, you're still paying because the fees are baked into the sales price. Why would you not want to have a true pro in your corner as you make your biggest investment? Some arrangements split the realtor fees and this arrangement is often contingent on the market practices of the area.

What Should You Look for in a Buyer's agent?

You may know a lot of real estate agents in your area. But keep in mind that not all agents bring the same knowledge and experience to the table. Don't work with an amateur just because they know your cousin's sister-in-law's best friend from ten years ago.

If you're trying to spend time with a friend or family member, catch up over coffee. Don't work with them to make your biggest purchase. You want an expert who can show you how to buy a home and get the best deal! When you're interviewing a real estate agent, don't settle. A true rock star will have:

- Specific experience assisting home buyers like you
- Full-time real estate experience for at least two years
- Great communication skills
- A servant-minded attitude that makes you feel like you're their only client
- An impressively long list of sold homes every year
- Exceptional experience in your local market

A true pro won't shy away from tough questions. They'll be a mover and a shaker, ready to fight for your best interests as you're searching for the right house and negotiating the terms of the contract. As a home buyer, working with a rock star agent is one of the biggest advantages you can give yourself!

Step 4: Go House Hunting

After you've been preapproved for a mortgage, you're ready for the fun part: finding your perfect home!

Once you reach this step, your finances should be rock solid, so you know exactly what you can afford. And with a real estate agent to guide you through the process, you have a winning combo for buying a home with confidence.

Before you dive into the home search, create a list of must-have home features. If you're buying a home with your spouse, make separate lists and compare. Once you have clarity on the features you both want, share them with your real estate agent and use those criteria as the foundation of your home search. Your agent will be able to help you set realistic expectations and target your search to areas you can afford.

How Can You Know You're Making a Good Investment?

When you're looking for the perfect home, it may be hard to imagine you'll ever sell it. But just remember, even if you think it's your forever home, you should shop with resale value in mind. Here are some home-buying tips to help you make a smart investment:

- Don't compromise on location or layout. These are two things you can't change about the home you buy. No amount of curb appeal can make up for a truly terrible floorplan. And buying a great house in a not-so-great neighborhood is a bad idea. If you don't love the location or layout, chances are, potential buyers years from now won't either.

- Look past the surface. Don't let a lime-green bathroom keep you from an otherwise great home. Other buyers may not be able to look past those easy-to-fix details like décor and paint color, which could score you a deal. That lime-green bathroom may mean more green in your pocket! I purchased my current house at a discount because the bathrooms were aged. Again, look past the surface for cost savings.

- Buy the least expensive home in the best neighborhood you can afford. That gives your home's value room to grow in the future. Keep in mind that future buyers who are shopping in a $200,000 neighborhood won't be looking for a $300,000 home.
- Pay attention to home values in that area. Are they rising or declining? Are businesses booming or closing? You can tell a lot about home values in a neighborhood by what's happening in the community.
- Research the school districts. Even if you don't have kids, school districts can be an important factor when you sell. Economists estimate that a 5 percent improvement in test scores can raise home prices by 2.5 percent in suburban areas.

The average homebuyer looks for about ten weeks before finding the right house, according to the National Association of Realtors. Don't sweat it if it takes you a while to find your perfect place!

Note on hot markets that routinely sell homes in 24 hours. You are sure to leave money on the table in these bidding war situations. These environments benefit the seller and only the seller. If that's your reality I simply request you proceed with extreme caution and not let emotion dictate your decision making process.

Step 5: Submit an Offer

Once you've found the right home, it's time to get serious! That means submitting an offer and signing a contract agreement with the sellers.

What's Included in Your Offer?

Your real estate agent will work with you to submit a solid offer. If you end up in a bidding war with other buyers, keep a cool head and put your best foot forward. Things like being preapproved with your lender and having a flexible closing date can help make your offer strong. Your purchase agreement will include details of the real estate transaction like the following:

- Buyer and seller information
- Property address
- Purchase price, lender information, and down payment amount
- Earnest money deposit
- Items to be left with the home (like appliances or furniture)
- Contingencies, like the home inspection, appraisal, and final mortgage approval

Closing Date

Sometimes, agreeing on terms is quick and painless, but it can also be one of the hardest parts of the process.

If your negotiations get intense, remind yourself that both parties want the same thing. The sellers want to sell their home, and you want to buy it. Sometimes it pays to compromise on little details if that will move the process forward. A good real estate agent can give you advice about when to give in and when to hold firm.

Step 6: Get a Home Inspection and Appraisal

Once you get to this step, you'll officially be under contract on your new home. That's something to celebrate! Being under contract also means you're done with the most time-consuming stages of the home-buying process. Cheers to that!

But now that you're under contract, what should you expect? Your main task now is to work through the contingencies in the contract. Contingencies are simply conditions that must be met for the home purchase to take place. They provide a safety net for you to back out of a sale without losing your deposit if something goes wrong. Even if you're in a competitive market, don't let your emotions lead the charge. You should never skip these contingencies because they offer important protections for your home purchase.

Home Inspection

As a buyer, you have the right to a professional home inspection before you purchase the house, and you would be crazy not to do it. This is one of the most important precautions you can take before purchasing a home because it keeps you from being blindsided by structural issues or expensive repairs. If the inspection reveals major problems with the home, you can ask the seller to fix the problem, reduce the price, or cancel the contract.

You can also consider getting other professional evaluations, like a termite inspection or radon test, depending on the advice of your real estate agent and the age and condition of the home you're purchasing.

Appraisal

If you're getting a home loan, your lender will require an appraisal evaluating the value of the property. An appraisal protects you from paying more than the home's true value. If the appraisal comes in lower than your offer price, your real estate agent can provide the best guidance for what to do next.

Final Mortgage Approval

The best way to pay for a home is with cash. Not only does it set you up for building wealth, but it also streamlines the real estate process. If you did get a mortgage, you'll have a final step before you can close on your home: getting final approval. Your lender will dig through the details of your finances to finalize your mortgage. Whatever you do, don't open a credit card, take on more debt, or change jobs once you're under contract. Plus, any changes in your financial situation can jeopardize your loan process.

Step 7: Close on Your House

You did it! All the planning, house hunting, and waiting are over. The final step in the home-buying process is closing on your new place! Before you get the keys for your new home and officially call it your own, you have one more sprint ahead of you: paperwork. That's right, bring on the hand cramps!

You should receive a copy of your closing documents to review ahead of time so there are no surprises on closing day. Most likely, you'll pay for the following:

- Closing costs
- Prorated property tax

- Homeowner's association fees (if this applies to your neighborhood)
- Homeowner's insurance

If there are any confusing terms or conditions as you work through the paperwork, don't be shy about asking questions. This is one of the biggest purchases you'll ever make, and you should know exactly what you're signing up for. Once you sign all the paperwork, it's time to breathe a sigh of relief. You're officially a homeowner, at least partially. Congratulations! The home-buying process may not be easy, but having a beautiful new home to call your own is worth it in the end.

The decision to buy a home is important, but so is the way you and your spouse go about making that decision and putting it into effect. This process can be a barometer to measure the health and maturity of your relationship. As you're exploring your options, take time to listen, understand one another, and pray together (if that's your bag) about your goals. Be willing to grow through the experience. Seek counsel from others—for example, a trusted friend that's been down this route before or perhaps someone that found themself upside down from a bad purchase. Take time to discuss your priorities and to talk about the pros and cons of buying a house. Don't jump into anything based on emotion, a desire to impress others, or an irresponsible penchant to spend money you don't really have.

Whatever you do, remember that purchasing a house is one of the biggest investments you'll ever make. Here are a few factors to consider in determining your readiness to take this major step:

Your Ability to Pay

Besides coming up with a down payment—which is essential—you'll need to figure out if you can afford the monthly mortgage payments. If you don't have a budget already, you should develop one to see how much money you actually have available for this monthly expense. (be sure to include taxes and insurance.) You can get a good idea of whether you're getting in over your head or not by using the following formula: first, divide your fixed debt by your gross income; then turn the result into a percentage by moving the decimal two places to the right. Most lenders want that number to be under 36 percent, preferably under 30 percent, and as close to 20 percent as possible (some will allow up to 45 percent, depending on your credit score.) Again, recommend your monthly payment represent no more than 20% of your take home pay.

"Forgotten" Costs

The costs of homeownership don't end with the mortgage payment. Some other expenses to keep in mind include fees associated with loan processing and purchase of the home; upkeep—everything from water heaters to roofs to painting; and property taxes and homeowner's insurance, both of which tend to increase over time.

Benefits (Long Sigh...)

On the positive side, you should remember that mortgage interest and real estate taxes are tax-deductible. For specifics in this area, consult an accountant or attorney who specializes in this field. Another benefit is the opportunity to participate in government programs that assist first-time home buyers. Then there's the simple value of ownership to be taken into account—the freedom to control your environment, remodel your house, put nail holes in the walls, or plant a garden without getting permission from a landlord. You will have to decide how much this is worth to you.

What if you decide you should buy a home but really can't afford it? In that case, there's just one thing to do: begin to develop a financial plan that lets you reduce or even eliminate existing debt. Freeing up money for a down payment and then building equity in a small home usually is a good long-term plan. Dreams can come true, but they usually require patience, perseverance, and time. Also, if you plan to get married, make sure you marry someone with similar financial objectives. I said it before and I'll say it again, reread that last sentence.

CHAPTER ELEVEN:
Liberation

Liberation: the act of setting someone free from imprisonment, slavery, or oppression; release.

MY WIFE AND I PAID OFF OUR HOUSE. Completely. As in, no more mortgage payments for the rest of forever. No debt of any kind, at all. Paying off my house in 2019 was one of the most liberating moments of my life, and I've been able to experience flexibility in my life choices because of it. When I sent in the last payment to the mortgage company, I looked at my wife in silent disbelief. I may have gotten a speck or two of dust in my eye.

This is how we did it.

1. We agreed on our goals.

After drifting into a sickening level of debt, I knew we'd eventually want some breathing room in our budget and thought the best way to do that would be to buy—and pay off—a house.

My wife agreed, and we embarked on geoarbitrage and moved to the Midsouth.

2. We paid cash for everything.

When we bought the new house, we used capital proceeds from our home sale in Colorado. All home upgrades were paid for in cash with savings. If we didn't have money for something, we waited until we did.

3. We bought less house than we could "afford."

The bank was willing to loan us more than double what we knew we could comfortably pay. So generous of them (snark, snark). We sat down and made a written budget so we knew exactly what was a reasonable house for us (reference What is a House chapter), and we bought exactly that much house and not a cent more. This is where having a good real estate agent will come in handy! You definitely want someone who respects your budget and wants to abide by it. In other words, someone who has your best interests at heart.

4. We drove used cars.

It seemed like all my coworkers and friends were driving shiny new cars, but we were still driving vehicles with love marks and LOTS of miles. I've made my opinions on luxury cars known, and we will continue to drive older cars that are paid off.

5. We kept a tightly written budget.

We wrote down on paper exactly how much we could spend each month on each category of expenses, and we each got a small amount of money to spend on whatever we wanted. We had specific budgets for groceries, utilities, eating out, insurance, and miscellaneous—discipline every single month. No exceptions.

The Joy in the Process
Freedom

I was shocked to find that this whole process of budgeting led to freedom. Before we set a budget, I felt a tiny twinge of guilt whenever I wanted to spend money on clothes or other random Amazon crap. This twinge of guilt has become a welcome friend that keeps me in my financial lane.

Peace

Having common goals brought my wife and I together in a huge way. There's nothing like setting goals as a couple, dreaming together, and getting on the same page to make them happen. We would lie awake at night and talk about what life would be like when the house was paid off. We would dream and plan together, and it was *so* good for our marriage. Because we made a financial plan, we never had to fight about what we were spending. Our priorities had already been decided, and now it was only a matter of following through. Eliminate the #1 reason for divorce - finances.

Hope

I know for a lot of people, times are tight right now, and I'm absolutely terrified that you will think I'm boasting. Hear me on this: I am thankful beyond words. God has blessed us. And we have sacrificed to reach this goal. I think you can do it, too;

I really do. It's HARD, and there's a lot of sacrifices there, but even setting small goals will give you hope, motivation, and space to reach for bigger things.

Now that we're on the other side of things and had time to let it soak in, one thing that's really struck me is this: I was happy eating peanut butter-and-jelly sandwiches as broke newlyweds with a massive mortgage. And I'm equally happy now being mortgage-free.

With that said, living life without a mortgage has eliminated one less stressor in life, but there will always be other stressors to address. It's one step closer to finding balance and contentment in life. It's not about how much you have. If you can't be content having little, you won't be content having more.

CHAPTER TWELVE:
Bring It

> The future belongs to those who believe in the beauty of their dreams.
>
> *- Eleanor Roosevelt*

We've covered a great deal, from macroeconomic trends to compounding interest, to geoarbitrage, to the euphoria experienced from owning a home. Like many other famous financial self-help books, let's break it down into a 7-step plan to living mortgage-free.

1. Commit to Mortgage Independence

You must believe living mortgage-free is an integral part of personal freedom. Otherwise, you will fail. When you think of debt and how mortgages make up the majority of personal debt, you must be relentless in your pursuit to eliminate it from your life. Debt is a prison.

2. Pay Off Revolving Debt First

Pay off credit cards and other sources of debt. In fact, don't carry balances in these buckets at all. If necessary, make sure it's for purchases that can't be paid in cash and ensure they are paid off in thirty to sixty days. Debt is a prison.

3. Buy Used

Buy used cars, furniture, clothes, electronics, and any other possessions. Buying new, while luxurious, will set you back from your homeownership goals. Debt is a prison.

4. Live or Move to a Cost-Effective Location

Live where housing is affordable. My home is approximately $100/square foot. This is why I could truly buy my house. If you're in a high cost of living area, consider the possibility of relocating. Debt is a prison.

5. Buy a Reasonable Home

Buy a home that can either be paid for in cash or can be financed under a fifteen-year fixed-rate mortgage. Remember, your mortgage payment should represent no more than 20 percent of your take-home pay. Disregard what a bank states you're qualified for—debt is a prison.

6. Educate and Give Back

Most of society has accepted mortgages as part of life. Reject this notion and educate others on the possibilities of living mortgage-free and financial wellness. Be an ambassador of the contrarian lifestyle and use your capital to make a difference in your community. Debt is a prison.

7. Recommit to Mortgage Independence

Never forget step 1, oh, and debt is a prison.

I sincerely hope this short book provided valuable tips and insights into living Mortgage Free by 40. If a putz like me can do it, so can you. I wish each of you all the best as you seek personal freedom by living a mortgage-free life. Go get it!

REFERENCES

1. Suzanne Fontaine, "Plan for Success in 2015," ProActive Pathways Consulting Inc., March 17, 2015, http://www.proactivepathways.com/.

2. "Take Charge of Saving in Your Forties," *Solutions for Financial Planning*, Winter 2015/2016.

3. Https://www.newyorkfed.org/microeconomics/databank.html

4. Https://www.magnifymoney.com/blog/mortgage/u-s-mortgage-market-statistics-2018/ https://fortunly.com/statistics/mortgage-statistics/#gref https://www.thebalance.com/how-does-real-estate-affect-the-u-s-economy-3306018

5. Https://constructioncoverage.com/research/where-residents-have-paid-off-homes

6. Https://www.theatlantic.com/ideas/archive/2020/01/american-housing-has-gone-insane/605005/?utm_source=pocket-newtab

7. Https://www.newhomesource.com/learn/how-much-square-footage-fits-yourfamily/#:~:text=The_percent20average_percent20size_percent20of_percent20new,to_percent20the_percent20U.S._percent-20Census_percent20Bureau.

8. Stacey Bumpus, "Dan Marino and 78 Percent of NFL Players Are Bankrupt or Broke," GO BankingRates, January 30, 2015, http://www.gobankingrates.com/.

9. Blake Morgan, "No Ownership, No Problem: Why Millennials Value Experiences Over Owning Things," Forbes, June 1, 2015, http://www.forbes.com/sites/blakemorgan/.
10. Canadian Press, "Canada's Debt-to-Income Ratio Sets New Record High at 165 percent," CBC News, March 11, 2016, http://www.cbc.ca/news/.
11. Jacob Poushter, "3. Social Networking Very Popular among Adult Internet Users in Emerging and Developing Nations," Pew Research Center, February 22, 2016, http://www.pewglobal.org/.
12. Gym Membership Statistics," Statistic Brain, December 1, 2015, http://www.statisticbrain.com/.
13. David Shum, "Price of Beer at Blue Jays Games 7th Highest in the League: Study," Globalnews.ca, July 23, 2015, http://globalnews.ca/news/.
14. Garry Marr, "Canadians Don't Just Love Home Ownership—They're Growing Fond of Income Properties, Too," Financial Post, January 26, 2015, http://business.financialpost.com/personal-finance/.
15. Lisa Wright, "Canadians' Monthly Car Bill: $437.48," Toronto Star, July 8, 2014, http://www.thestar.com/business/.
16. Ron Lieber, "Paying Tribute to Thomas Stanley and His 'Millionaire Next Door,'" New York Times, March 6, 2015, http://www.nytimes.com/.
17. Jason Heath, "The Upside of Higher Rates," Financial Post, March 31, 2012, http://business.financialpost.com/personal-finance/.
18. Rob Carrick, "The Hidden Trap of Mortgage Penalties," Globe and Mail, December 5, 2013, http://www.theglobeandmail.com/globe-investor/.
19. Kimberly Amadeo "Real Estate's Impact on the US Economy" December 1, 2020, https://www.thebalance.com/how-does-real-estate-affect-the-u-s-economy-3306018

20. Samantha Rose "10 Eye-Opening Financial Literacy Statistics—OppLoans" March 18, 2021 https://www.opploans.com/oppu/articles/statistics-financial-literacy/

21. How 5 Common Types of Amortization Can Impact You [+Definition] (lendingclub.com)